The Lore and Lure

of the Coastal Banks

Love,
from Porter and Billie

by

Billie Jean Huling

Billie Jean Huling

The Lore and Lure of the Coastal Banks

Billie Jean Huling

Mount Olive College Press
Mount Olive, NC

Library of Congress Catalog Number: 93-77741

ISBN 1-880994-19-4

Published by: Mount Olive College Press
Mount Olive College
634 Henderson Street
Mount Olive, NC 28365

Printed by: Spectrum Printing Company, Inc.
Route 8, Box 301
Kinston, NC 28501

Illustrations by: Beth Munden

*To my two sons who inspired me to write
poetry when they were children.*

PEN AND INK ILLUSTRATIONS

The pen and ink illustrations of the artist, Beth Munden, were created especially for this book and are unique in their relation to each poem.

BETH MUNDEN, Artist
Carteret County, NC

ACKNOWLEDGMENTS

The author acknowledges with gratitude the cooperation of editors in whose publications materials herein have appeared:*Golden Summers,* copyright 1991, by **VOICES OF THE AMERICAN PEOPLE,** and copyright 1991, **THE MAILBOAT,** Coastlore; *Tomorrow on Bogue Banks,* copyright 1992, Anthology: **SELECTED WORKS,** World of Poetry Press; *Little Banker Pony, Golden Summers,* and *Vow,* copyright 1991, **THE MAILBOAT,** Coastlore; *Thistle Down,* copyright 1992, *Poems from the Crystal Coast,* published by The Kiwanis Club; *Thistle Down,* copyright 1992, **HERE'S TO THE LAND,** an anthology compiled by the North Carolina Poetry Society; *Sun Sparkles on the Sound,* copyright 1992, the Mailboat Christmas Book, **CHRISTMAS KIN.**

The author would like to thank Dr. Pepper Worthington for her editorial guidance, encouragement and leadership. With her help through the Mount Olive College Press this book has become a reality: *The Lore and Lure of the Coastal Banks* now a part of the North Carolina collection at UNC-Chapel Hill's Wilson Library.

TABLE OF CONTENTS

THE LORE AND LURE OF THE LAND

THE LORE AND LURE OF THE PEOPLE

THE LEGACY:
TO THE CHILDREN OF THE BANKERS

PALLADIAN WINDOWS

THE LORE AND LURE OF THE LAND

Beth Munden '94

GOLDEN SUMMERS

Between Bogue Banks and the rolling surf

there lies an Emerald Isle.

Emerald she's called, and emerald she is,

but a golden isle to me.

There I count my years by summers,

summers spent by the sea.

Between the Sound and the raging sea

lie the sand and the clear blue sky

where gulls are mewing and sand crabs scurry to hide;

where suds from the surf run up from the sea;

and shells from her depths crunch under my feet;

where waves come in slow motion to soothe and talk to me.

Between Bogue Sound and the rippling sea

my life is wild and sweet,

and my heart is as pure and as full of dreams

as the ocean is wide and free;

where the world of commerce is quite unknown,

and the world of fantasy holds the key.

13

(The Ushers of a Coastal Fall)

The ushers of fall descend upon the merkle bushes near the edge of a Sea Level marsh like thousands of yellow flecks falling into the tasty berries. They come swirling through the pine tree forest amid the swiftly-falling needles, their tiny chirps hardly heard, as they return to herald the cooling autumn. They have scouted the grape arbors and fruit trees to find nothing left of summer's bounty as they swoop down, driven from the Artic and Canadian blasts, and now at last settle in to survive again. Those avid foragers of food sample th sowllen blue-gray *merkle* berries and carry the fat and pungent *bayberry* seeds to begin anew another clump, tending their life cycle and our own.

Poised at the portals of marsh, foragers and planters, they outwit all the other birds, tend their life cycle, then return north at the first hint of spring to begin a new life cycle there.

THE MARITIME FORESTS OF THE BANKS

The live oaks of the Banks bend and sway together,

      for there is might and warmth in such unity.

But on the oceanside trees have been salt-mist sprayed

      until they stand stark and gray with helpless limbs.

Now the sands drift and mud flats appear where a great

      maritime forest once stood.

This is a virgin forest living in the hearts and minds of

      the Bankers.

It is a bulwark soon to be living only in the annals of the

      Banks and in fond memory.

A tree was only one tree, but a maritime forest, living and

      thriving, ensured security of the Bankers.

TURNAGIN BAY

It's the turning of the seasons in the coastal marsh.

> Take me back, take me back to *Turnagin Bay*

> where we used to net mullet from our boats near a cay.

It's the turn of the seasons and I'm drawn homeward now.

> Take me back, back again to *Turnagin Bay*

> where breezes stir purls in the deep-water bay.

It's the turn of the seasons. My mind sees it all.

> Mullet charged by the season jump into my boat,

> which we'll charcoal again on a home-made grill

> and taste their sweet meat from the laid-back skins.

There will be passing V's of the southern-bound ducks

> with a few drawn back to the washes below,

> just as I am drawn back by a magnetic drive

> to the turn of the seasons at *Turnagin Bay*.

Reliving the past turns me homeward again

> to that old wooden boat as it bobs at the dock.

Take me home once again to *Turnagin Bay*

> where I may see old friends at their nets in the Bay.

BOGUE BANKS

Between Bogue Sound and the raging surf

    lies a thread of purest sand,

    unspoiled, untamed, and teeming with beauty of the land.

Between the banks and the islets lies a safe, calm cove

    where the loneliest of coast guard stations

        guards this treasure trove;

    where the dunes rise up and shelter the loons;

    where eel grass and sea oats hold the dunes;

    where small game and birds abound to fill summer nights

        with an eerie sound;

    where scrub oaks grow twisted and blown toward the land,

        buffered and massed by the blowing sand.

          Enjoy it now, marvel at the dunes.

          Record the wild-life sounds

for a trail is cut to the end of the strand

and we fear that progress may ruin our land.

THE SAND DEVIL OF WINTER

Dodge the whirlwind of the sand devil,

      as he whirls and twirls like a holy dervish,

      twirling with religious fervor.

Chase the wily sand devil,

      whining with the howling wind,

      like the dervish with his reed pipe,

      merging mind and being as one pure soul,

      searching for the meaning of the sea.

Just as the winds of March create him,

      and he stirs dusty devils in his wake,

      earth awakens, whirling, twirling, surging

      with new life, and the bursting buds of spring

      swell, revolving with the source of new creation.

SURVIVAL

There is eternal magic in the coastal plants:

> Live oak scrub, buffered and blown
>
> by the raging winds toward a calmer smoother Sound
>
> like the sturdy old fisherman, weathered and worn.

Palmetto palms struggling to survive

> in a border-line climate, brown and rustling
>
> in the early March breeze in the same way that a
>
> displaced one struggles to fathom the Southern mind.

Spanish bayonet trees which grow in banked sand,

> spiked and knifed, pointed for the thrust
>
> like the evil hand grasping white crested flowers in
>
> one hand, sword in the other, symbolic of the careless
>
> lover, selfish in his need.

Wild myrtles, called *Merkels,* waxed and waiting for

> warblers in fall by the marshes of wire grass near
>
> sea oats to devour, characteristic of spongers on the
>
> largess of humanity.

Sea oats which shatter as the wind finds the dune,

> scattering and lofting nature's seed above,
>
> planting and seeding when others fly by, just as the
>
> coastal farmer overplants to fulfill his needs.

Cattails on ditch banks, proud and tall,

      with lush brown coating over feathers of down

      which are carried as clouds to reseed the Banks,

      significant as the dreamer whose vision reaps

      final rewards.

Tall pine trees of magic with needles of mulch

      to multiply and replenish the soft sandy earth.

      Adaptable as sandspurs, they filter the sand,

      and thrive upon weakness of poor coastal land.

      They are buffered and blown, like the aging fisherman

      whose small leaky boat hauls a full fish net.

A clump of cactus called coastal pear pads await the

      unwary with needles of pain. Their sweet yellow

bloom buds attract eager hands that find vials of poison

      awaiting instead. This wild one resembles the

      dashing sailor with pretty words but sly intent.

Despite nature's ravages, these wild plants still prevail.

RIDE THE COASTAL WINDS

November is the pause before winter's deep sleep,

    when the lack of light brings the deep depression of

    death.

Gardens stand stark and unkempt awaiting a far-off spring

    as dried seeds and stalks rattle in the winter wind.

Seeds snuggle deeper into the cool moist earth awaiting the

    fruition of time as their internal alarm clocks await

    the spring.

Savage winds begin their sweep across the sounds, and burning

    sands attack our bodies like cutting glass.

Wild geese emit their wilderness cries from distant flight

    as the sharp bark of the skittering fox sounds at

    the marsh's edge where scaup huddle together on Core

    Sound.

Two swirling flocks of blackbirds merge as one, as if seeking

    the warmth of numbers. They part, ripple, and surge with

    an almost sexual frenzied merge.

Now the churning winter winds sweep and throw balls of foam to

    run up the sandy beach.

Temperatures drop and the silver fingers of ice are caught up

    in the marsh reeds as prisms of light are suddenly

    revealed by an unexpected winter sun.

The days move swiftly as winter grasps the coast with the
fierceness of its claws.

We welcome the sharp whip of the winter winds, knowing we
must endure yet another damp coastal winter, so that the
warming lap of our waters can swirl around our feet once
more as the tides surge and flow toward the eternal
rhythm of the coastal seasons.

PROMISE OF A COASTAL WINTER

As surely as winter is reached in the coastal wash,

    rain and dry leaves will freeze against cold panes.

Plaintive bird cries and the honk of geese will signal

    the arrival of winter.

Rafts of mallards drifting toward a littoral will huddle

    together for a semblance of warmth and security to

    signal the stirrings of change.

Schools of mullet and bluefish retreat from the frothing

    turbulence into the deep, dark depths of the ocean

    to hide from winter's freakish nature..

Otters cease to play their friendly gamboling games, and

    quietly slip away.

Gulls drop oysters, partake of tasty bits, and leave

    their refuse, as they skim away.

All these seek the safety of barrier isles just as we

    seek safe havens of the mind's scope to escape

    life's winters.

PROMISE LAND

The earth's seething core of eternal alarm sounded the progression of time on

Shackleford Banks;

    When the littorals shifted, sifting the sands of time;

    When the backbarrier marshes ceased to evolve;

    When salt-sheared vegetation lifted ghostly arms heavenward;

    When even the cistern water turned salt;

    When the water witches and *merkle* warblers fled, leaving only scavenger

gulls to forage;

    When the tombstones fell over, and their words could not be read;

    Then and only then were we forced to leave for the *Promise Land* to find

a *proper place.*

It was like a step into the dark, plunging into a vast, black unknown.

We sailed into darkness, for our roots were deep in sand of the Banks.

We fled

like the Indian maiden auctioned as a slave

for $50 in Beaufort.

She could not be forced

to keep the kitchen or to work the fields of Carteret.

THE LAST TWO LEAVES ON
THE DOGWOOD TREE

The last two leaves hung lifeless on the old dogwood tree like rumpled, crumpled paper, waiting for another Spring.

First, they had flourished, lush and green, among a bower of burgeoning trees.

They were buffered and blown by the April showers, then blistered and dried by the torrid sun.

Fall blew through and burnished them gold, coloring them dark with garden smoke.

One by one the others fell until the world was a rubble of trampled leaves beneath our feet.

Yet, two still clung to the tree of life.

Winter drew near and birds savaged seeds stripped in seconds from the dormant tree.

Still, two leaves clung in the cold and sleet, emerging from snow to crumple beside our feet.

One was ninety; the other, only one hundred and three.

Two more leaves to bury beneath life's dogwood tree.

Two immoveable and immortal souls, left by our Lord to light our paths; two lovely leaves left on the old dogwood tree.

THE SONG OF KATHERINE

Our little wren must fly away,

       soaring to heights above the clouds.

No cage can hold her spirit now.

       Its bars are broken, thrown away.

She filled her world with love and care

       until her turn to fall to ravages of time and tears.

It's been so long since she was caged by mental chains that

       held her bound and physical ills to test her strength.

She never ceased to fight the odds, our fragile bird with

       songs unsung, but now her words are clear, her voice

       pure, as she joins the Heavenly Host in song.

Today our little bird with drooping wings will lift them up

       and soar into her Lord's embrace.

CHANGE AND CONTRAST

Between Bogue Sound and the mighty sea,

      the waves come in slow motion, serene, and never ending,

      or raging wild from storms just out of reach.

      The suds from the sea run up the beach in foaming froth.

How I long to go, to cross the sound, to laugh and sing,

      as we did long ago when the Banks were ours alone;

      but the tentacles hold, and the tentacles bind —

      two worlds that can never meet.

Now summer's end is coming to both the isle and me,

      to this work of nature and the world of childish dreams;

      for a trail now cuts this narrow slip of isle;

      and we fear the many changes pending.

Beth Munden '94

SUN SPARKLES ON THE SOUND
The Ca'e Banker's Creed

On the fourth day, after the Lord of the Universe had made the sun to shine upon the Banks, He cast sun sparkles on the water to shimmer like so many precious diamonds glinting on its surface.

Then Man was brought forth in clouds of sand. He told the Lord:

"This is good. I will claim all the fish that swim in the sea."

The Man heard thunder from the cloud banks and the Lord's precepts:

"Man hath dominion over all living, creeping, and swimming creatures. Take care to protect them as I protect you."

As time passed, Man and creatures multiplied upon the earth, and the creatures began to fear nets of the sea and traps of the earth.

Man strayed and forgot his God; he grew sad and quarreled with his friends; he grew lonely and felt forlorn.

In desperation, the Ca'e Banker prayed and gazed again at the sparkles on Bogue Sound.

Those same sun sparkles reminded him of the Lord's Might and Power to inspire hope and peace within his lost and struggling life.

Then the Banker renewed his stance and moved with the ebbing currents of the sea and his life.

VOW

Someday I'm leaving the shore behind.

Someday soon, I'll be ready —

Ready to leave the slashing waves,

Blind to a *"slick ca'm"* sea.

Someday Lookout will not mean much

With her history of whalers wild and free.

Someday I'm leaving it all behind —

Away to the thrill of the city's grind.

I'll be a spoke in the city's wheel

If its charms should so entice.

But for now the lore of the coastal banks

Still holds me in a vise.*

Someday I'll go when I'm tired of the sand

And the water's lure of shrimp and shells,

When wild banker ponies may leave me cold.

I'll go when I'm tired of the history of Macon,

tired of the fishing and the swirling waters,

When Carteret's riches are fully partaken.

Let's face it, not fight it,

I'm a Carteret *latecomer* who's here to stay.

Someday I'll go, as nature intends,

Alone into darkness seeking the light,

Where it glows with warmth of my Carteret friends.

*A vise or vice is a clamping device used in carpentry or metalwork to hold a piece in position.

THE LORE AND LURE OF THE PEOPLE

Beth Munden '94

THE FORGOTTEN TOMBSTONES
OF THE BANKERS

On many abandoned islands along the mighty sea

> are simple gravestones of the Bankers whom hardship set

> free.

Some of the stones can hardly be read but names were copied

> lovingly before our people fled.

Storms and tides have challenged terrain, and ghost trees stand

> in mute control at the edge of maritime lanes.

There are Shackleford and Portsmouth, Shell Castle, Dollar, and

> others we cannot name.

Their people fled the wasteland to homes across the Sound to find

> a *proper place* in their *Promise Land.*

The neatness of nature, an inborn sense of earth changes, the

> dawning of a fresh new life, the sinking sands, the storms,

> the shifting of moon tides, and the beauty of the sea

> remind them of the ancient rhythm of the universe.

This is the path to life's change and renewal for the Bankers of

> yesterday and today.

Beth Munden 94

THE CA'E BANKER'S BENCH

The Ca'e Banker sits on his old Banker's bench.

It has weathered soft gray by the salt-laden air.

His nets are all gathered around his bare feet as

       his shuttle flies swiftly so the mesh will then meet.

His dim eyes peer at a long-distant past

       when the fish were abundant along Ca'e banks.

He dreams of his youth of vigor and might,

       of man-powered boats and whales in the Bight*.

He longs for salt mullet, for robins and loons.

He is waiting alone for his daughter's call

       to hard crabs and *dumplins* like his mate used to make,

       or to oysters and clams he has taken by rake.

He lives all alone. She left long ago to sleep

       in the graveyard under totems of conch,

       where they hang from the branches of green live oak.

There she rests forever among her own folk.

He strokes the gray wood of the solid old bench.

It has weathered by time like the Banker himself.

His roots are all buried so deep in the sand,

       he will never stray far from his bench on this strand.

*A bight is a bend or curve especially in a shoreline.

COMPEERS

Small towns and country roads —

    these I've always loved.

The first was Gap Town in the hills,

    where I was always shy and poor.

Why did I love it, you might ask?

           My friends were living there.
           You should know who you are.

But then, I worked in a busy city not far away.

    I loved it too, the courts, and law books

where I learned my place in its musty halls.

    Why did I care for something quite dull?

Because my friends were there, you know.

           They cared for me, I care for them
           You do know who you are.

    And then, I chose a different path

and followed my heart to the Ashepoo.

It was isolated but so beautiful there,

like a dream, with a crushed-shell road,

    with isles in flower and camellias everywhere.

           But best of all, we made friends there.
           You know which friends you are.

But stars are crossed and full moons come.

    Our own careers were so diverse.

You must move up, and so move on,

    so off we went once more,

to mountains, seashore, and research across the sea.

                  We left our friends so close.
                  You know just who you are.

    I've never lived in a place I did not love

for its unique and lovely sights,

    for the friends I've made, and good times shared.

I treasure and revere each one,

    You are friends like alter egos, compeers of fine rapport.

          You know which friends you are.

DREAMER'S ESCAPE

Depression's Child:

In ragged coat and holey shoes,

      she smiled and chased the butterflies.

On vacant lot with old tin cans,

      she watched soft thistle blooms,

      and chased their *fairies* when the breezes blew.

She watched the hen upon her eggs,

      and climbed the tree for a last red plum.

She found a hill where four-leaf clovers always grew,

      and picked them for her pickle jar at home.

      Good luck, she knew, in every one.

And then, so very slowly the Great Depression went away.

War and the Girl:

"The country is invincible," they said,

      "no one would dare to challenge us,"

      but soon her friends went off to war.

      The war required first place.

Their food was scarce, and times were hard.

      War work for all, able or not.

Some friends were lost and presumed dead.

      Her tears were held within.

The girl could only wait and hope,

and dream of better days.

She watched the birds and fields and streams,

and read and wrote her verses then.

But then, so happily did it come — *Peace in our Time*

once more.

The Woman and War Once More:

A global war has come to us from far across the sea,

with the U.N. now involved.

"Where will it lead us now?" we plead,

"A germ and nuclear war?"

Our finest fly forth to the Gulf.

Our sons may follow Dad to war.

She watches and hopes for a swift peace,

and contrasts this war with another one,

when he first went forth to fight.

She shudders, cries, and fears their fate,

as she recalls the past.

She starts a journal of these days

and writes to soothe the pain.

She watches birds and flowers in bloom,

the ocean and the sound,

and finds a four-leaf clover for her vase.

She does research and writes her book

       to ease the fear and pain.

Do we need a war beyond control

       to make us see what matters?

She folds her hands and breathes a silent prayer

       for each and every one.

PICTURE FRAME

You stood beneath the old live oak

    like a mighty athlete proud and bold.

Your arms akimbo, your legs apart,

    you painted a picture in my heart.

The years are shattered; we both move on;

    but a fond mind picture is living there.

The frame was frozen, set in time,

    as the years are slipping, one by one.

I think of watching surf and dune,

    and sometimes quietly watching you.

We walked the beach so long ago,

    my hand in yours as I worshiped you.

I wish our lives had never changed,

    that we could stroll that stretch of sand,

    and you still stood within that frame.

DERVISH

I write with a dervish on my shoulder,

       a whirling, twirling devil there,

       chanting, circling with religious fervor,

       always prodding, always pushing absolute perfection

       with his barbed pitchfork.

There he dances, a minute, but mighty demon.

       I would reach him if I could.

       By his frenzied antics, he evades me

       as I strive to feed his ego, while he's laughing,

       leaping with his barbed pitchfork.

"Write," demands the dervish, prodding:

       "Use your talents, or you lose them!"

       "Who are you to flirt with death?"

       "Time allotted you is fleeting," chants the dervish

       as he twirls just out of reach.

CREATIVITY

A block of wood, a bar of gold,

a bit of stone, a metal cast —

These are tools to be used by a creative mind

in a labor of love through the seaman's hand.

A speck of oil, a pot of paint,

a canvas roll, decking smooth —

These are complements used by a skillful hand

for beauty to share with all mankind.

Pieces of wood, hammer and nails,

plans from memory stored away —

These are the substance of life-long dreams

launched by action of the sailor's hand.

The cold winds will shriek across the waves

to find him intent upon winter's task

of building a boat with flare and style

from plans his daddy sketched on the wall.

This is my friend, a man of perception,
who is driven to seek illusive perfection.

The joy he feels in the boat's completion
is unrelated to its years in creation.

RIP TIDE

Once when I was young and foolish,

in a moment of despair,

I let a wave engulf me and carry me elsewhere.

Then a voice within me challenged:

Swim with the tide, don't panic.

Don't fight your world or the wild Atlantic.

I count my years by moments since that lonely, sad,

lost day, and live each day with happiness

as I give myself away.

PERCEPTION

My Dear Old Friend in the Brotherhood of Poets:

You asked why we still write poetry.

The answer seems quite clear.

It's in our perception of objects and events.

I see a bird indelible upon my memory,
with every feather, beak, and song,
as it was more than forty years ago.

I see the creek, each rock, and trout,
clear, clean, and pure as it was then.

I see the homeplace, paths, and pond
in glowing, living color just the same.

I see the beauty in photographic memory.

I turn and see the ravages of accident and death,
of illness and suffering as it was then.

I see the war and hardships too,
the loss of my dear friends without a body to inter.

I smell the fear and churn anew to know the pain of a
child alone, hurt by those who profit from their greed.

I can't forget the hurricane that drove us forth
to start anew, the loss and shock therefrom.

We're just alike, the two of us, my friend:

imbued with a talent we must express.

It is a blessing to see the beauty through the years,

a curse to face the pain anew with each remembrance.

So, we must write to walk the tightrope of today.

TOMORROW

When I am old and my senses are dim,

      I'll live on the Banks that have sheltered me.

I'll sit on the beach and throw in a line.

      Never mind the fish, for I'm half blind.

I'll sit outside and feel the sun,

      or search for shells with just my toes.

I'll feel salt water on my arthritic bones;

      and when there's a storm, it will match my moans.

I'll be all alone, I'm sure about this,

      for who could fathom this sea-swept cove?

I'll reach in my fish bowl filled with shells

      and pull out the memory that each one tells.

So I'll waste not a moment, keep wide-open eyes,

      hear all sounds of nature, and smell salt air,

      live and be happy and watch the parade.

Sad days may approach, but memories won't fade.

Beth Munden '94

WHEN THE LIGHTS
WENT UP IN BEAUFORT

Where have they gone this Christmas Eve?

> The menhaden fishermen at their nets, fishing for the
> silvered slivers of fish, their sea chanties lost upon
> the wind. Here and gone, those coastal men, strong and
> virile, pulling nets with their cadenced measure. They
> were Carteret and Onslow men with roots deep in the
> coastal sands, loath to venture into water beyond the
> beckoning Gulf Stream, but it was their livelihood. It
> was Christmas Eve and many were aboard the boats at
> Beaufort. That December the stacks at the fish
> factories had belched forth the odor of new money, for
> the catch was abundant off Carteret shores.

Saddened by being so far from home, I was chastened as I saw a myriad of
lights sparkling in reflection across the water from Piver's Island. The
fishermen, far from home, had mounted live cedar trees in the crows' nests
atop the boats. The lights, powered by the generators of the boats, lit our
hearts and created a Christmas far from home.

> Gone now are many of those stalwart men, filtered
> through the hourglass of time, leaving only fractured
> sparkling memories of the night when the lights went up
> in Beaufort.

Beth Munden '94

ICE MOON OVER THE MARSH

This is the last quarter of the Ice Moon when ice hangs
      on the marsh reeds, sparkling and reflecting earth
      thoughts of the long night.
See the curled leaves of the live oaks with their
      stretching limbs sprung to sever the crusted ice
      and the long-leaf pines creaking and splintering in
      the naked cold.
It is the time to dream of shore birds drawn from the
      marsh in rafts and vees to their northern homes in
      anticipation of an early spring.
It is a time for warm lightard-knot fires* and warming
      drinks before its warmth. It is the time for
      pursuing mind-picture dreams among the flickering
      feathers of flame.
It is a time for the Banker to count his stacks of wood
      in anticipation of the shortening winter's need.
It is a time of reflection and regret, for resolutions
      and absolutions; a time to anticipate the spring
      yet savor these moments when the Ice Moon casts its
      spell as reflected through the ice crystals of
      winter.

*A lightard-knot fire is one of pine knot with pitch. The knot burns long and well and is tough to cut up. Because the pine knot is full of pitch, the fire is hot.

It is the time to see an ice rim on Peltier Creek as the
warm Gulf Stream undulates far out to sea and the
giant old pelicans huddle on the pilings of the
creek.
All are waiting within their cocoon of time to welcome a
changing of the Ice Moon.

ONE THREAD

Poetry is the thread that holds together

the fragments of my life:

The lonely years of a dependent child;

The fractured verses penned to ease the pain;

The struggle of between years for meaning and identity;

The fast-paced life of one with two careers;

The jig-saw puzzle of the middle years; and

Finally, the sunset years and time to sing the coastal

song waiting to be sung.

One thread throughout.

THE LEGACY:
TO THE CHILDREN OF THE BANKERS

THREE BROWN PELICANS
AND A LITTLE BLUE CRAB

As three hungry pelicans scanned the beach, a little blue crab told them sagely:

Fly, big pelicans,

fly to the sea.

Plunge in the water where you see the spray.

Dive deep and seize those silver kings;

flip the fish above your bill;

then face the wind as it whips toward shore.

Go meet your flock and ride the wind,

wingtip to wingtip to look for more.

There are fish to catch, shrimp there too.

You can't eat me; my shell is too hard.

THE CHILD'S VIEW OF THE COAST

Roots in the sand.

Chains in the sea.

"What do you mean?" my child asked me.

Feet in the sand.

Heart in the sea.

"That is possible," a man told me.

The wise old Banker once said:

You have captured the Spirit of the Coastal Banks.

I thought about those words, then felt I must reply:

No, the Spirit of the Banks has captured me.

It's a magnetic lure that binds us together

once we partake of the riches of coastal shores.

We cannot go home; we cannot leave.

The Bankers are bounded with feet in these sands.

The fishermen are boundless with skylines to scan.

There are shipwrecks to salvage by *wrackers* * at sea.

If you share their lifestyle, you may never leave.

*Wrackers comes from wrack, a noun meaning wreckage, especially a ship cast ashore. A wracker is one who salvages from the wrack or wreck.

THE KITES OF MACON

The kites are gathering at Fort Macon Beach.

    --red, yellow, purple, and blue.

They dip, they dance, and seem to laugh

as they tease their masters just out of reach.

There are box kites, bubble kites, square kites,

and diamond kites that dip and gabble on their own.

Gypsies from far across the sea are thrilled.

They laugh and point to the kites with delight

as the light marsh breeze carries them out

into the blue skies far over the sea.

The travelers are dancing just like the kites,

dipping and prancing, clapping and laughing.

What will they remember when they return home:

hustling, bustling, non-caring delights,

or a picture in the mind's eye, a simple sight

in a far-away land, the colorful kites of Macon,

--red, yellow, purple, and blue,
dipping and dancing, flipping,
and laughing?

PENNING OF THE LITTLE BANKER PONY

A Tale of Core Banks

You can't go home, you'll have to stay,

    Sang the lonely lad to the little bay.

No more you'll roam the Banks and Ca'e,

    For they say your breed must be fenced away.

His head was down and his mane was matted,

    And he felt defeat though his pen was slatted.

He saw blue water, sniffed salt air,

    And dreamed of a freedom beyond the Bar.

Dimly he knew how his sires had come,

    Over the seas with pirates and rum,

Up from the Santo where left by Balbo,

    thence to the Banks by Teaches' foe.

The evening crept in and the moon was on Core.

    Little Banker was quiet, but grieving no more.

Low tide was approaching as he swayed to and fro.

    The fence gave quietly and he hung his head low.

He snorted as he ran with no place to hide,

    And made ready to swim at the ebb of the tide.

The men came running with shouting and flame,

    But the little Banker Pony was riding to fame.

    He splashed and he swam to Shackleford Bend

To run free and wiry, and strong to the end.

Now he'll flee and he'll hide when men come to fish,

or lads hunt for turtles by the moon if they wish.

He'll watch from a distance, or sprint out of sight,

When they come for a ride, or may give them a fright.

PHOTOGRAPHIC MEMORY

There stands the child at the old seaman's knee

      hearing his tales of life upon the Banks.

Beware of that child with the apple cheeks

and frightened green cat eyes.

The child is quiet and well behaved.

      Take care! Speak softly and beware.

She sees mind-pictures set in time

      to soft and lovely music.

Those pictures are forever etched

upon her quick and sensitive mind.

Her poetry is transposed and moves in time,

      living in the winters of her life.

Those pictures are indelible, concealed behind the lens;

      pictures that speak of life beside the sea.

One day the child will poise with pen in hand,

then write.

Beware, young man, your life is written there!

OLD MAN LEV*
A True Story

There lived an old man on Morehead Shore

    who cared for the graves on the Calico.*

He dug those graves and cut the weeds,

    travelling fast from row to row.

But Old Man Lev grew old and weak.

    He needed a rest from all those dead.

He bought a lot and built a vault

    and climbed inside to make his bed.

Now Old Man Lev worked on and on, older and older

    with an afternoon rest, where none dared enter,

    disturbing the dead, till late one day,

    lads chanced on his nest.

They awakened Old Lev from his deep sleep;

    and he sat straight up with a mighty roar.

UP FROM THE GRAVE HE AROSE, shrouded in an old white quilt.

    From the depths to the heavens, he seemed to soar.

The lads dropped their gear and fish they had caught

    and ran for their lives from a ghost so close.

They screamed and they cried of what he had wrought,

    and they told everyone FROM THE GRAVE HE AROSE.

Beth Munden '94

The years rolled by and they found Lev cold

    so they buried hm in the vault he had built.

When the boys sneak through, they have often been told

    Old Lev will awaken; but if they are bold,

    THEY WILL SEE HIM RISE UP FOR ALL TO BEHOLD!

* Lev is pronounced "Leave."
* Calico Creek is named for the Calico scallop found there. The cemetery is on Crab Point Road.

EIGHT O'CLOCK WHIP-POOR-WILLS

We sat in our bower under live oak trees

  draped in damp moss with yellow-green leaves

  in an isolated area on a tide-land river,

  which wound through the marshland east to the Sound.

As we waited and listened, one opened his trill:

  Poor-Will! Whip-Poor-Will! Whip-Poor-Will!

  Our watches were set by their eight o'clock call,

  which seemed release of a scheduled chorus.

As a car drove through the darkening night,

  their glowing red eyes seemed sinister and bright.

  they rose up before it, ghosts in disguise

  like many red coals from a cauldron below.

HAMMOCK'S BEACH

"Have I ever been to Hammock's Beach

across the flip-flop waves?"

inquired the lad of the *question marks.*

"Yes, once as a child strapped to my back

we trudged up the highest dune

and came to the mighty rush of a storm-swept beach."

I answered him.

It's an island like no other,

lonely, wild, and windswept.

Approach by ferry sets your mood.

The islets between shield the leggy crane, the awkward grebe,

and the fly-way birds destined to pause and rest.

The boat swings into the sound-side dock

where mountainous sand dunes rise before the eyes.

You must be a hiker to reach the ocean side.

It's a barrier isle with a reason for being there,

a breeding ground for the wild ones, never a home for man,

only habitat for God's great roaming creatures,

three pelicans and a crab.

So may we go again, my son and I, to Hammock's Beach,

his strong hand on a trembling, spotted, ancient one.

FEE FAH'M MULLET BLOW

I knew a lad named Juba Lee.

      He lived in the Low Country close to me.

Juba would fish in Fee Fah'm pond

      on an old rice farm returned to the wild.

The leaves were blowing, the water roiled,*

      when Juba spied the trap with ropes re-coiled.

The squills and gumbo were pushed to the top

      by a mullet blow down White Shell Road.

The fall mullet blow caught Juba Lee

      as his wire fish trap bobbed near the sea.

An old wooden boat was wedged in the lock

      where the fish were jumping, so they leapt in the boat.

The fish were caught as forced in the trap

from the rising tide in this strange mishap.

They jumped from the lock into the boat

      and Juba jumped too, when he saw the weird sight.

He laughed, and he pranced, for he could not stay calm

as he filled several sacks at old Fee Fah'm.

He carried his fish up White Shell Road

and fed *his 5,000* in that mullet blow.

*Roiled is a verb which means to make muddy or cloudy by stirring up sediment. Water roiled is in a state of turbulence.

RABBIT TALES

I doubt myself when I tell this tale,

    but it's true, so help me to tell it straight.

We drove up Shell Road past the double twin lakes

    past the swamps and 'gators lounging in wait.

We saw a fat cottontail crossing our path.

    All his legs were churning like four little wheels.

He froze in mid-air, as we laughed, and you said:

    "His legs are still going, just think how he feels!"

Now where is his mate, in slow motion too?

    And what of their bunnies down in the lair?

Will they outsmart their enemies,

    if they freeze in mid-air?

Was this freak of nature a plan to survive

    through a ploy of that rabbit

    to stun and ensnare an enemy fox,

    one not quite so wise, just a creature of habit?

THE WATER WITCHES*
OF BLACK WATER

Dip and surface,

> Dap and dabble,

Spear a minnow,

> Swallow him whole.

Clothed in magic by the ancients,

> Watchful eyes scan every move.

Spells and spinnings,

> Myth and magic

Drawn from Africa's sunless depths.

Called Di-Dappers by the boys,

> Called the *witches* by the ancients,

As they circle with their magic,

> Skimming low across the water.

When the 'gators lounge too close,

> Witches tempt their fate alone,

Spinning circles of black magic.

> If they pause, they flirt with death.

*In the South Carolina Low Country, the grebes are called Di-Dappers, or Water Witches, as they ply the black pre-historic waters of the back marshes. In the coastal areas of North Carolina, they lead a more secure life. Dipping and gliding, they are called *di-dippers*, but even in those marshes, they are often subject to the whims of predators.

79

HARBINGER

Hummingbird, hummingbird, where have you flown?

You've brightened my garden while I was alone

      with your ruby red throat and your green satin back,

      your wings making cartwheels, never contact.

Red attracts you, and trumpet flowers.

Red flowers especially are your favorite lairs.

Hummingbird, hummingbird, in a land of strife,

I see dark clouds and fear for your life.

It's a gray, cruel world we live in,

      a world which we have made.

The smog is especially heavy in our glade,

      and a pall has settled on the strand.

We struggle to breathe as we fear for our land.

I fear, little pet, you lie limp in a nest,

      a nest that looks like a fragment of trash;

      or did your bright spirit dim in wildest flight

      as you reached for an opening with all your might.

Hummingbird, hummingbird, bright good-luck charm,

      our flowers droop and wither, as we feel our alarm.

But, look! a ray of the sun, after days of gloom,

The pall should lift, as does the bloom.

You will return. Of this, I am sure.

Bright harbinger of hope, you found escape

      and soared to heights of pure, clean air.

THE SHELLS OF SEA CASTLE ISLAND

Your Legacy

Crunch the shells beneath your feet;

listen to their music.

Pick the shells for perfect treasures;

gaze at all those subtle hues.

Scan them closely for their value;

smooth and rigid, round, or strange.

Think of creatures building castles.

Do they rival human efforts?

Hold them tightly in your fingers;

turn them over in your hand.

Look at them with wonder.

Teach your children:

all their fables, how the ocean roars within.

Show them how to build a memory

in a mirror or a picture.

Relate all their ancient history

from creation of the oceans

to the Indians.

Tell them of their places in the chains deep in the sea.

THE *MERKLE* WARBLERS

Down from Alaska frozen and iced,

      Trooped the warblers to warmth of a salt-water marsh,

      drawn to the myrtles by an instinct of nature,

      where the round fat berries sustain their life.

      They are called bayberries for they grow near the bays,

      where birds hover all winter 'til the first warm day.

      Then splotches of yellow on whirling brown wings

      are seen fleeing northward to greet a new Spring.

HERITAGE OF FORT MACON

The mighty Fort of Macon guards this outlet to the world,

      as the history of Fort Macon lives on in memory

      with gray ghosts skimming over marsh and sea.

Its massive doors and moat that shield it guarded soldiers

      stationed there, now only shimmering shades weaving over
      marsh land waste.

The ghoulish shadows in the arched brick doors remind us of

      Confederate soldiers, the guardians of Fort Macon's fate.

Seeking light to guide our steps, we slide upon the slippery floor,

      and smell the molding walls within her inner gate.

The water drips interminably as it did when it was new

      and we feel the strange malaise which caught her inmates in
      their fitful sleep.

We see a cannon ball wedged in the forward wall and marvel that

      it is preserved intact.

Emerging from its dungeons dark and damp below,

      we break into the sunshine and climb soaring steps

      to a higher vantage point.

We see the marshes, inlet, and the booming, roaring surf.

We view the town of Beaufort where ancient cannons

      shelled this solid fort.

Where are those men of Macon so alive in memory

      Do they lie forgotten in an unmarked site or were

      they tossed below at sea?

      Would they believe that we remember and honor those below

      when we mount the parapet of history and hear the bugle blow.

FORT MACON

Macon is a magical place, never tiring, ever changing,

 filled with the rhythm and poetry of life,

 cloaked in history, some alive, but more forgotten.

 Home to great brown pelicans moving in perfect harmony,

  moving on currents, swooping down dunes,

 Home to busy sanderlings and the sandpiper birds,

  scurrying and feeding on coquinas left by the tide.

Macon lies off the inlet, gateway to mysteries of the sea,

 where ships we can see, ships at sea, more than a thousand

 ships at sea.

From Macon We See:

Beaufort Inlet:

 With large and small sailboats and dinghies,

 kayaks and motors, freighters and liners,

 ships at sea, ships at sea, more than a hundred

 going far out to sea.

*The Mighty
Atlantic:*

 Mystical, never tiring, ever changing, crashing

 waves and wind-tossed froth, storm or calm,

 and always ships at sea, ships at sea,

 more than a thousand ships at sea,

seen from Macon, tossed by the sea.

Bird Shoal:

Banker ponies and marsh grass, sea birds, and
scavengers, and always the undulating tide,
sweeping in and out to foreign ports,
more than a thousand ships at sea, seen from
Macon, moving out to sea.
Always changing, always new, always magical and
compelling, always filled with the rhythm and
poetry of life and of history, changing,
changing, filled with music of the water and the
natural beauty of the sea.
Ships at sea, more than a hundred ships setting
forth to sea, rushing half-way around the world,
Ships at sea, again making history.

THE KITTIWAKES OF CARTERET

The kittiwakes of Carteret are testing the waves.

Stranded by hundreds on shifting sandbars by the storms at sea near Emerald Isle, the kittiwakes of Carteret are calling:

"Kitty, wake. Kitty, wake!"

The ocean is turbulent; the winds are sharp as they are held captive by a magnetic force.

Huddled in warmth of sun on sand, these most-favored gulls search for darting minnows in the minute ponds.

Awaiting a calm in the turbulent seas, they watch for fishermen and follow their lead.

They attract attention by their graceful swoops and dive under water from high spiraling loops.

This wonder of nature will seek Arctic cliffs to parade their beauty and continue their breed.

The kittiwakes of Carteret will soon return, searching for fishing boats and calling your name:

Kitty, wake. Kitty, wake!"

THISTLE DOWN

The vacant lot was littered with cans,

      but weeds obscured the trash.

A blue-eyed toddler peeked over the spire

      and spied the beauty there.

The tendril spikes of purple silk

      perched inside cups of green

      first caught her quick and sensitive eye

      as she teetered on the fence.

The summer flew by and ripened the seeds.

      The shimmering wind caught up their silk,

      wafting away on wings of down

      to the rich bottom land east of town.

She cupped her hand to catch the sprites

      but grasped the thorns instead.

With a shock she learned how pain is hidden

      in the beautiful summer of life

      encased in a heavenly magic stalk.

THE DI-DIPPERS OF DUDLEY'S POND

Down near the marshes on a secluded pond

      live nine di-dippers with a common bond.

The dip and dive with head below,

      leaving only a triangle of tail fluff to show.

They feed in a frenzy on small tasty bait,

      and elude alligators just lying in wait.

They rise with a whir when he floats nearby,

      teasing to snare them as they rise with a cry.

Around and around in widening puddles,

      they swim or float in islands of huddles.

The lively di-dippers in the icy rime

      are swimming and playing as if in mime.

They ply to the music of a waltz in time,

      dipping and diving in circles of nine.

PALLADIAN WINDOWS

PALLADIAN WINDOWS OF MY SOUL

Each prism of thought, each impetus of moral fiber,

    each flood of emotion influencing man's vital core,

    filters like a thousand fragments of light

    reflected on the stained-glass windows of my soul.

They are elements forged into the vital core of my being,

    immortal, but separable, at my wilted body's demise,

    my sole legacy and my only gift of good or evil

    in a sphere fraught with man's inhumanity to man,

    reflected through the Palladian windows of my soul.

BILLIE JEAN HULING

ABOUT THE AUTHOR

Billie Jean Huling was born at Big Stone Gap in the Appalachian mountains of Virginia. She and her husband, Porter B. Huling, Jr., moved to Morehead City in 1965. They have two sons, Robin C. Huling and M. Ross Huling.

"Carteret County is one of my favorite places in the world," said Ms. Huling as she began to explain her reason for writing about the lore and lure of the Coastal Banks. "I have not captured the spirit of Carteret County as much as the spirit of Carteret County has captured me," she declared.

What appeals to Ms. Huling are Bogue Banks, the ferry rides to Ocracoke, Oriental and Cape Lookout; the rich sea life of shells, sand, pelicans, crabs, loons, cranes; the history of Fort Macon; the colorful kites during warm summer days.

"I have been inspired by the spirit of the people of Carteret County," said Ms. Huling. "They are independent, self-sufficient, respectful. They believe in the land and the sea."

Ms. Huling writes both poetry and prose. To her, poetry is the purest form of language. "When I work with poetry," she explained, "I am more aware of making things visual in the shortest number of words. Poetry helps me tighten my fiction."

Ms. Huling has published prose and poetry in *North Carolina Poetry Society Collection, Here's To The Land; Coastal Plains Poetry Society, Coastal Plains Poetry; Kiwanis Clubs' Poems From The Crystal Coast (1991, 1992); Selected Works Of Our World's Best Poets: Poetic Voices Of America; The Mailboat; Presbyterian Advent Publication, In Our Midst (1991, 1992); Christmas Anthologies By The Mailboat, Remembering Christmas Past, Our Christmas Memories, And Christmas Kin, Carteret Country News Times, and Mount Olive Review.*

Carteret Couny artist Beth Munden has drawn pen and ink sketches to illustrate numerous poems in Ms. Huling's new book. Of Beth Munden's work, Ms. Huling observed, "I find her talent unique. Her sketches have a feeling. When I see one of her coastal scenes, boats, pelicans, or flowers, I immediately recognize *her* work. Her pelicans are humorous, and all her birds seem real as if they are about to jump out and land in your hand," she said.

"Beth Munden is a native of Carteret County and she has a feeling for the spirit of the coastal banks. This brings rapport for the two of us," added Ms. Huling.

Currently Ms. Huling is polishing her novel, *Beneath the Devil's Nose.* The story takes place in the coal mining Appalachian mountains. Devil's Nose is a rocky projection in these mountains that looks like a nose. The novel keeps coming back to that image, as if the Devil's Nose is symbolic of the mountain area, its strong people who are self-reliant just as the coastal people.

"Appalachian people and coastal people are similar in temperment. They are alike and yet they can't relate to each other. Mountain people are bounded by the mountains. Coastal people are bounded by the banks," she said.

Ms. Huling has been working on her novel for 40 years. The historical span of her story is from the end of World War I to the end of World War II.

"But my first love is the lore and lure of the coast," she concluded. "And Beth Munden's three chubby pelicans looking at a blue crab captures both the humor and mystery of the coast.'"